AUSTIN MAHONE

By Marie Morreale

REAL
BIOS

Children's Press®
An Imprint of Scholastic Inc.
New York Toronto London Auckland Sydney
Mexico City New Delhi Hong Kong
Danbury, Connecticut

Photos ©: AP Images: 24 top (Charles Sykes/Invision), 22 bottom (Evan Agostini/Invision), 34 (Liz Condo/Sprite), 43 center top right (Nick Wass), 23 (Robb D. Cohen/Invision), 21 bottom (Todd Williamson/Invision); Dreamstime: 38 top right, 39 top left (Danny Hooks), 20 (Fitimi), 15 center left (Glenn Nagel), 41 top left (Sbukley), 43 top right (Zhukovsky); Everett Collection/20th Century Fox Film Corp.: 15 top; Getty Images: 18 (Aaron Davidson), 27 (Alberto E. Rodriguez), 4, 5, 43 center bottom left (Alexander Tamargo/Clear Channel), 8 (Bruce Glikas/FilmMagic), 26 (Christopher Polk/TAS), 31 (Ethan Miller), 29 (John Parra/Univision), cover (Juan Aguado), 41 top right (Larry Busacca/MTV), 17 (Larry Marano), 14, 44 (Larry Marano/Clear Channel), 43 bottom left (Mike Coppola), 6, 7, 32 (Paul Warner/WireImage), 12 right (Tasos Katopodis/Clear Channel), 41 center left (Taylor Hill/FilmMagic), 2, 3 (Timothy Hiatt/Radio.com), 43 center left (Uri Schanker), 43 center bottom right (Valerie Macon); Landov: 9 (Coolpix/Barcroft Media), 1, 25 top (Manuel Nauta), 38 bottom (Mark Blinch/Reuters); Newscom: 16 (Christopher Peterson/Splash News), 30 (Derek Storm/Splash News), back cover (Dzaa/Zds Wenn Photos), 21 top (infusmi-13/INFphoto.com), 42 (Manuel Munoz, PacificCoastNews), 25 bottom (Mayer RCF/Splash News); Rex USA : 36, 37 (Masatoshi Okauchi), 41 center right (Picture Perfect), 43 bottom right; Shutterstock, Inc.: 15 bottom left (Aleksandar Groz), 13 center (aperturesound), 13 top (Bloomua), 39 bottom left (cobraphotography), 39 bottom right (Costi Iosif), 12 left (CrackerClips Stock Media), 22 top (Debby Wong), 40 top, 40 center top, 43 top left (DFree), 15 bottom right (dibrova), 11, 15 center right, 43 center top left (Helga Esteb), 24 bottom (Jaguar PS), 40 center bottom (JStone), 41 bottom (My Life Graphic), 38 top left (Nonnakrit), 39 top right (Rishiken), 35 (Rose West Photo), 40 bottom (s_bukley), 13 bottom (S.Borisov); Thinkstock/iStock: 38 background and throughout, 38 pushpin.

Library of Congress Cataloging-in-Publication Data
Morreale, Marie.
  Austin Mahone / by Marie Morreale.
    pages cm. — (Real bios)
  Includes bibliographical references and index.
  ISBN 978-0-531-21377-3 (library binding) — ISBN 978-0-531-21430-5 (pbk.)
1. Mahone, Austin, 1996– —Juvenile literature. 2. Singers—United States—Biography—Juvenile literature. I. Title.
  ML3930.M27M67 2015
  782.42164092—dc23 [B]   2014031107

Printed in the United States of America 113

SCHOLASTIC, CHILDREN'S PRESS, and associated logos are trademarks and/or registered trademarks of Scholastic Inc.

1 2 3 4 5 6 7 8 9 10 R 24 23 22 21 20 19 18 17 16 15

MEET AUSTIN!
HE'S NO LONGER A SECRET!

Do you have an Austin Mahone poster in your room? Have you downloaded *everything* from his YouTube cover songs to his **EP** *The Secret*? If you answered yes to these questions, you are an official member of the Mahomies— and proud of it! It also means that this *Real Bio* is a must-have. Get ready to meet Austin's family and BFFs and check out his favorite snacks, songs, and superheroes. Best of all, you'll experience Austin's rise to stardom in his own words. It will make you smile . . . and maybe even laugh!

Austin loves touring because he gets to meet his fans, the Mahomies!

CONTENTS

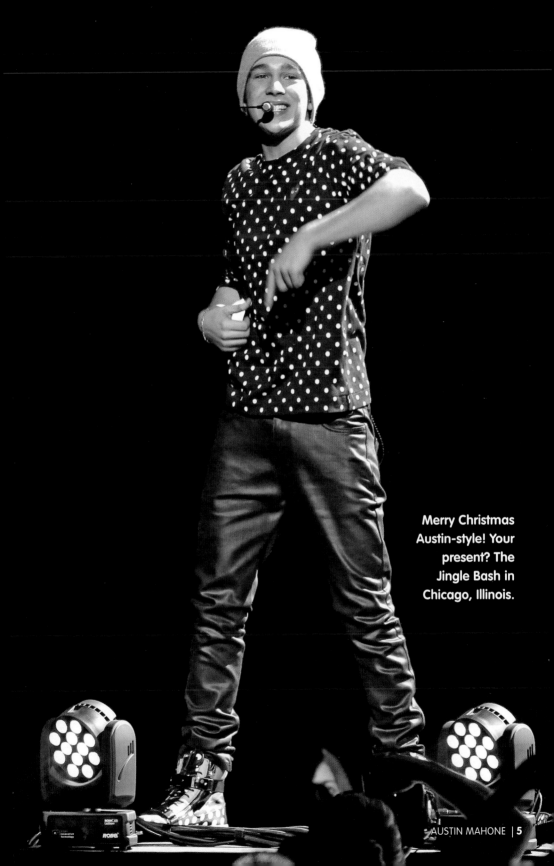

Merry Christmas Austin-style! Your present? The Jingle Bash in Chicago, Illinois.

AUSTIN MAHONE

SHY GUY TO SIGH GUY!

YOUTUBE, SKYPE, TWITTER, & FACEBOOK CREATE A SUPERSTAR!

Born on April 4, 1996, in San Antonio, Texas, Austin Carter Mahone was a much-loved baby. But when Austin was less than two years old, his father died. Austin's mom, Michele, became a single parent who had to work and raise her son at the same time. She got a job at a local bank and worked her way up to the position of mortgage loan officer. However, there were times when Michele and Austin faced difficulties.

"It was just me and my mom," Austin told *J-14* magazine. "I grew up very close to her. . . . Of course we struggled. I never had to share a room with my mom, but we lived in a small apartment. It just had two bedrooms, a living room, a kitchen, that's it."

Michele taught Austin what was really important in life—family, education, and setting goals. There weren't a lot of extras in the Mahone home, but they had everything they needed. Austin shared a perfect example with *J-14*. "When I was little, I didn't get everything I wanted on Christmas or my birthday," he said. "I would have a long list, you know every kid wants everything, but it's all too expensive. [But] my mom always made each holiday special and that's what's really important— family and spending time with them."

Austin's mom encouraged him in all his interests—sometimes to their neighbors' horror. "My first instrument was drums and I started playing when I was 6, and then I played guitar

Austin's mom, Michele, is his best friend and adviser.

Advice from Mom
"There are so many things she says to me, but I would definitely say to 'stay humble' is the best."

at 14, [and later] piano," Austin told Scholastic Web site The STACKS.

The music sparked something in Austin. "The more I [played] music and practiced those instruments, the more it just felt like this is what I wanted to do, like that's what was . . . supposed to happen for me."

Fun in the sun with Austin and his best buds! Don't you wish you were there?

For a while, Austin's love of music was an inner dream. He had other things on his mind—like fitting in at a new school when he and his mom moved to La Vernia, a small town outside of San Antonio. They moved because Michele had remarried. Unfortunately, that marriage ended in divorce. Austin and Michele stayed in La Vernia for a short time before going back to San Antonio to live with Austin's grandparents.

"I've never been the most confident person," Austin confessed to *Twist* magazine. "Since I was two, when my dad passed away, it was just me and my mom. We'd been doing our own thing since then, and when we moved to a little country town, I was different from everyone else. They were all dressed country with boots, jeans, cowboy hats. They always hated me and made fun of me. They picked on me every day for two years."

Luckily for Austin, he found some classmates who were like him. Austin connected with Alex Constancio, Robert Villanueva, and Zach Dorsey. "I had my group of friends [who] were similar to me, that were from the city, so we had each other and we would just help each other get through it," Austin explained to *PopStar!* magazine.

When Austin and Alex started watching goofy videos on YouTube, they came up with a smashing idea—to make their own crazy videos and post them online! In the summer of 2010, they created their own YouTube channel, ShootUsDown. "The first video was us fighting in [Alex's] bedroom," Austin told *Details* magazine. "We were just punching each other."

YouTube King
"I saw other people on YouTube making covers and I thought it was really cool and I just wanted to try it."

Austin and Alex soon graduated from **vlogs** of them fooling around, going one-on-one on the basketball court, and generally acting like clowns. Music was the replacement. Because Austin was the one with the musical talent, they decided to post him singing **covers**

Austin and his long-time friend Alex Constancio share a moment.

of popular songs by major recording artists. In October 2011, Austin uploaded his very first YouTube cover—Justin Bieber's "Mistletoe." He soon posted covers of music by artists such as One Direction and Drake. Much to his and Alex's surprise, they started getting followers. To promote their YouTube channel, Austin and Alex went to the mall and passed out flyers. They also spread the word through friends at school. Whenever a fan posted a comment online, Austin wrote a response. In a matter of weeks, they had more than 20,000 dedicated fans, and the list was getting longer and longer.

Things changed at school, where Austin was once a "nobody." "People came up to me in the school hallways," Austin told *Details*, "people I didn't know, telling me, 'Wow, you're so good, please post another video.'"

The first time Austin performed in front of an audience was at a school pep rally. "This cheerleader in my school asked me to sing . . . at the rally," Austin recalled to *Twist*. "I really didn't want to. She also didn't tell me that it was . . . a singing competition! I ended up singing and at the end the MC put his hand over the head of each person who sang, and there was some cheering. But when he got to my head, the crowd went crazy and it felt really good. I knew I should sing then."

As Austin's followers grew in number, he reached out to them more and more. He

THE BASICS

FULL NAME: Austin Carter Mahone

NICKNAMES: AM, A-Meezy

BIRTHDAY: April 4, 1996

ASTROLOGICAL SIGN: Aries

BIRTHPLACE: San Antonio, Texas

CURRENT RESIDENCE: Miami, Florida

MOTHER: Michele Mahone (Mama Mahone)

PET: A cat named Romo

HIGH SCHOOL: Lady Bird Johnson High School

BEST FRIENDS: Alex Constancio, Robert Villanueva, and Zach Dorsey

MUSICAL INFLUENCES: Justin Bieber, Drake, Ne-Yo

SECOND LANGUAGE: Spanish

CELEBRITY CRUSHES: Mila Kunis, Rihanna

FIRST CAR: A red Range Rover

TECH TOY: Two iPhones— one for business and one for personal calls

LUCKY NUMBER: 74

LITTLE-KNOWN TALENTS: Can wiggle his ears and play the beatbox

FANS' NICKNAME: Mahomies

BEST CHRISTMAS PRESENT: A guitar

started performing at fan parties and special events near his home. Then he started traveling to other states to perform live shows—and he was paid for them! "I promoted myself on Twitter and Facebook as hard as possible, nonstop," he told *Hollywood Reporter.* "People started realizing that if they commented on my videos, I'd reply to their comment, so I started getting a lot more views and comments. . . . I tried to connect personally with the fans as much as I could to make them feel like it's one-on-one, even though it [was] like one-on-500,000."

FACT FILE

FAVORITES

SPORT: Basketball

NBA PLAYER: Tim Duncan of the San Antonio Spurs

TV SHOWS: Family Guy and A.N.T. Farm

SONG TO SING IN THE SHOWER: "Let Me Love You" by Mario

PLACE TO RELAX: The beach

U.S. CITY: New York City

SINGER: Drake

COLOR: Red

ANIMAL: Tiger

SUPERHEROES: Batman and Superman

TEXT MESSAGE ABBREVIATION: (:

SCHOOL SUBJECT: English

BOOK: The Time Machine by H. G. Wells

INSTRUMENTS: Guitar, drums, and piano

OUTFIT: Basketball shorts, T-shirt, and a cap

SHOES: Kanye West's Air Yeezy 2

VIDEO GAME: NBA 2K

SOCIAL MEDIA: Twitter and YouTube

ROLE MODEL: Justin Timberlake

Soon, Austin and Alex came up with the idea to offer fans Skype meet-and-greets. "I thought it would be cool to Skype with fans on their birthdays and spend like a half-hour with them. I did a couple of two-hour Skypes. I just hang out with them and play songs and stuff. At first they're kind of shy, but after a while they open up. I've had a lot of people tell me I'm doing something no one has ever done before."

All the money they earned through performances, appearances, and merchandise went right back into their "business." But more than money, Austin was becoming rich with fans! It was around then that they came up with the idea to create a nickname for their fans, like One Direction's "Directioners" and Justin Bieber's "Beliebers." "I'm just so blessed to have so many fans," Austin told 4Music.com. "I call them my 'Mahomies.' I actually came up with it myself . . . when I was sitting in my room with [Alex] and we were talking about all these crazy fan names that people have. So we

Mahomies line up for the *Today* concert!

Blinded by the light! Cell phone photos of Austin onstage are priceless!

were like, 'If we had a fan base one day, what would we name them?' And I came up with 'Mahomies' for mine and I guess I told someone and word kind of spread."

Word did spread, but not only to fans. Soon the music industry was calling. Michele realized this was serious business. She quit her job to handle Austin's career. **Gigs** and promo events were nonstop. Then Austin signed with a Miami-based management group, Chase Entertainment.

Impressed with Austin's social media numbers, the managers introduced him to radio, brought in **producers** and writers, met with record labels, and set up shows. All the hard work paid off. In 2012, Austin signed with a label, and he was ready, willing, and able to meet stardom head-on!

Austin shows off his moves while performing at SunFest in Palm Beach, Florida.

AUSTIN PROVES HE'S NO BABY BIEBER

AWESOME, ADORABLE, AMAZING!

Austin quickly learned that there was a lot of hard work involved in a music career. Because he had already won a huge audience through YouTube, Twitter, and Skype, record companies were interested in him. Kara DioGuardi, the former *American Idol* judge, wanted to sign him to Warner Bros. Records. She told *Hollywood Reporter*, "He knows how to connect. I think people feel attached to him because he's so genuine."

Unfortunately for the other record companies, Team Austin eventually decided to sign with Republic Records, home of superstars such as Drake, Florida Georgia Line, Ariana Grande, and Lil Wayne. It was a great business decision. But the move from San Antonio to Miami wasn't easy for Austin. When he and his mom first arrived, they thought Austin would go right into the studio. But that's not the

Sweet Tweets
Austin has more than 7 million Twitter followers.

way things are done. First, Austin's managers had to find him the right songs and cowriters to work with. Then they had to match him with the right producers. After a while, Austin began to get antsy. "I think about it all the time," he told *Hollywood Reporter*. "When is stuff gonna get done? I wanna move forward, not sit in my room like I do every day."

Well, Austin soon got his wish . . . and more! On February 14, 2012, Austin gave his fans a perfect

> "I JUST WANT TO MAKE [SURE] EVERY SONG . . . IS PERFECT."

Valentine's Day gift—his first single "11:11" was released, and DJs all around the country were swamped with requests for it from Mahomies. When Austin released his second single, "Say Somethin," on June 5, the video quickly racked up more than 1.5 million views.

Suddenly, Austin's career was becoming hot, hot, hot. Teen magazines had Austin on their covers. Major music

Austin's Timeline

Follow Austin's Climb

JUNE 2010
Austin posts his first YouTube music video

SEPTEMBER 2011
Austin debuts on *Billboard*'s Social 50 chart, becoming the youngest performer ever to do so

Imagine what it's like being in Austin's video for "Say Somethin"—these Mahomies can tell you!

magazines were writing articles calling Austin the "Baby Bieber" and predicting he could have the same meteoric rise as the Canadian pop star. That comparison wasn't how Austin wanted to start off his career, even though Justin Bieber was one of his favorite singers. "Justin's inspirational," he told *Details* magazine, "and it's flattering to be compared to him. It's cool. But I don't

FEBRUARY 14, 2012
Austin's debut single, "11:11" is released

JUNE 5, 2012
Austin's second single, "Say Somethin," is released

AUGUST 28, 2012
Austin signs a record deal

APRIL 27, 2013
Austin wins the Breakout Star award at the 2013 Radio Disney Music Awards

Austin salutes his fans at a *Today* Rockefeller Plaza concert.

want people to see me as a copy of Justin Bieber. Sometimes I can't breathe without being compared to him. If I wear a certain hat: Justin Bieber. Wear a certain shirt: Justin Bieber. It's so annoying."

Not long after Austin made that comment, the newcomer met the pop prince in person! It was around the time Austin was promoting his third single, "Say You're Just a Friend," and he was in New York doing back-to-back appearances and interviews.

JUNE 4, 2013
Austin's first EP, *Austin Mahone,* is released in Japan

JULY 25, 2013: Austin appears as himself on the Nickelodeon TV show *Big Time Rush*

AUGUST 25, 2013
Austin wins the Artist to Watch award at the MTV Video Music Awards

While making a visit to DJ Elvis Duran's Z100 show, Austin bumped right into Justin, face-to-face. "I got in an elevator, and he was standing right there," Austin told Celebuzz.com. "He was a really cool dude. The advice that he gave me was that it doesn't matter how successful I get. I just gotta keep going and not be like, 'I made it here so I'm gonna stop working hard.' I gotta keep working harder and harder."

SideKick
Austin's red guitar is always with him onstage.

   Austin took that advice to heart. As a matter of fact, during his interview with DJ Elvis Duran, he mused about success. "People don't really know . . . they think success is just a straight line . . . but if you really think about it, it's more like a squiggly line that goes all over the place. Getting ready for shows, making songs and just trying to get the hits out there . . . people

NOVEMBER 10, 2013
Austin wins Push Artist and Artist on the Rise at the MTV EMAs

NOVEMBER 28, 2013
Austin rides in the Macy's Thanksgiving Day Parade

JANUARY 24, 2014
Austin releases "Mmm Yeah," the first single from his upcoming EP

FEBRUARY 24, 2014
Austin headlines MTV's Artist to Watch tour

think that you put a song out there one day and it blows up the next. Everything takes time."

Nothing like a selfie with Austin! Smile!!!!

Austin spends a lot of that time reaching out to his fans. By 2013, he had way too many fans to Skype with all of them. Instead, Austin became one of MTV's favorite guests. On February 7, he debuted the "Say You're Just a Friend" video on MTV.com and then took over the @MTV Twitter account to answer questions from Mahomies.

MAY 1, 2014
Austin wins the Instagram Award at the iHeart Radio Music Awards

MAY 26, 2014
Austin packs the *Today* plaza with screaming Mahomies and debuts his latest single, "Shadow"

Then on June 10, he stopped by "Live from MTV" and just hung out with the lucky fans in the audience. He talked about his new video "What About Love," told the fans that his go-to dance move is "the glide," was challenged to do 30 push-ups in 30 seconds, and had a pie-eating contest with two fans. What fun!

Believe it or not, Austin loves to teach his fans his dance moves!

Besides having a great time with fans and dropping single after single, Austin had some other pretty big news in 2013. He was asked to be an opening act for six dates of Taylor Swift's Red Tour. That was a pretty big invitation for a young singer, and Austin knew it. When he got the news,

MAY 27, 2014
Austin's second EP, *The Secret,* is released and hits the number one spot on iTunes

JUNE 5, 2014
Austin sings the national anthem at the first game of the 2014 NBA Finals

JULY 25, 2014
The Secret tour kicks off in Austin's hometown, San Antonio, Texas

AUGUST 10, 2014
Austin wins Choice Music Breakout Artist at the 2014 Teen Choice Awards

Ed Sheeran, Taylor Swift, and Austin share a moment while they are on the Red Tour.

"I was speechless," he told Elvis Duran. "She's one of the biggest artists in the world and she's actually one of the nicest girls in the world, too. It's incredible."

Austin told JustJaredJr.com that he was excited "just being able to perform for 70,000 people. I've never performed for that big of a crowd before. I'm not really sure what to expect because I've never been on tour before, but I think it's going to be fun. I've been rehearsing for a while now, just getting ready to do the shows."

So on May 4, 2013, Austin took the stage in Detroit for his first night on the Red Tour. It was just the beginning of the whirlwind for him. On July 17, Austin learned he was nominated for MTV Video Music's Artist to Watch award for his video "What About Love." He told MTV News, "It's a huge honor to be nominated for Artist to Watch. It means I'm getting noticed out there and I'm getting that exposure. I'm pretty excited and I really can't wait to go and hang out. . . . It's so incredible because I can remember back in like, 7th, 8th grade . . . I would be supposed to be doing my homework, but I would stay up watching the VMAs, just admiring everyone on the show. It's really cool to be on the other side for once."

On August 25, Austin realized it was well worth the wait. It was the night of the MTV VMAs. Austin and Ariana Grande each took to the preshow stage to entertain the crowds. And then the pressure was on. Austin was up against Twenty One Pilots, Zedd, The Weeknd, and Iggy Azalea for the Artist to Watch award—and he won!

To top it all off, Austin got to meet his idol, Drake, for the first time backstage at the awards show. Austin tweeted, "Finally met my favorite artist last night! @Drake so good to meet you bro. I hope we can work together in the future."

Newcomer Pia Mia shares something with Austin— they both got their start on YouTube.

Just days after he won the VMA, it was announced that Austin would be headlining MTV's Artist to Watch tour starting on October 17, 2013, in Miami, Florida. In an interview with MTV News, Austin could hardly contain his excitement. "It's really cool," he said. "I've been in the dance rehearsals for a couple of weeks now just getting ready. I've gotten more dancers. I've gotten more songs I'm adding to it, so, you know, we got like lasers and lights and smoke. It's gonna be a huge production, so I'm really excited . . . so it's gonna be a really fun tour and I can't wait."

Everything was going great—and then it all screeched to a sudden halt! Instead of heading for the Miami stage to kick off his tour, Austin had to make a detour to the hospital. The entire tour was postponed, and Austin's mom tweeted

AUSTIN CELEBRATED HIS 18TH BIRTHDAY WITH A GIANT KEYBOARD-SHAPED CAKE!

all his fans, "Hey Mahomies its @michelemahone Austin is very ill. Unfortunately we are going to have to postpone the entire MTV Artist to Watch tour. Austin is very upset about this & we want to say we are sorry to all the Mahomies & their parents who have made arrangements to come out. We feel very bad but we have no choice but to POSTPONE the tour for now. Thank you for your prayers #PrayforAustin."

The official cause for his hospital stay was explained by Austin's representatives: "[Austin] was admitted to the hospital with 104 temperature and is being treated for a blood clot and extreme inflammation in his throat, as well as severe dehydration."

Pitbull and Austin hang out at a music event in Miami.

When Austin was released from the hospital, he wanted his Mahomies to know that he was feeling fine. "The doctors said it was probably caused by not having enough rest, not enough exercise, and not eating right," Austin told *J-14*. "I'm getting better every day."

The tour was rescheduled to a nine-city run from February 24 to March 9, 2014. In the meantime, Austin had to get rest and relaxation. Of course, that was easier said than done. He was up for two awards at the MTV Europe Music Awards—Artist on the Rise and Push Artist! "To be nominated alongside such awesome people [including Ariana Grande, Cody Simpson, Lorde, Imagine Dragons, and Iggy Azalea]) was crazy," Austin told

Brrr! Austin was chilly at the Macy's Thanksgiving Day Parade—but warm-hearted for his fans!

TeenVogue.com. "I just am so thankful. It feels crazy that I won, and that I won two awards!" Next came an appearance with Ariana Grande in the Macy's Thanksgiving Day Parade and nine Jingle Ball appearances. When 2014 arrived, things didn't slow down. In early January, Austin had three concerts in Japan, where he ate sushi for the first time! Unfortunately, while he was in Japan, he missed the 2014 People's Choice Awards—he was nominated for Favorite Breakout Artist, up against Ariana Grande, Imagine Dragons, Icona Pop, and Lorde. This time Ariana won. Luckily, Austin was back in the United States to participate in the Super Bowl week festivities—he performed at a free concert in New York City's Bryant Park.

On April 4, 2014, Austin celebrated his birthday by giving his Mahomies the best gift of all. He tweeted,

"IT'S TRUE!!!! MY DEBUT RELEASE #The Secret COMES OUT on May 27th!!! . . . AND MY FIRST BIG HEADLINE TOUR STARTS ON 7/25!! . . ."

Austin and Cher Lloyd announce a Billboard Music Award for Miley Cyrus!

Austin also announced that he was giving his Mahomies the chance of a lifetime with MTV's Ultimate Fan Experience. On May 3, fans could enter online to win a chance for a private dance lesson—for themselves and three friends—from Austin's dancers, a makeover, and a possible chance to perform onstage with Austin during his upcoming tour.

Another award? You bet—Austin won the Instagram Award at the May 1, 2014, iHeart Radio Music Awards. The winner was chosen by fans.

On May 27, *The Secret* was released and shot to number one on the iTunes charts.

"I CAN'T THANK MY MAHOMIES ENOUGH. THIS IS ALL BECAUSE OF THEM."

Austin looked ahead—tours, albums, more meet-and-greets . . . and more dreams to come true!

ASK AUSTIN
ANYTHING!
CHECK OUT WHAT HE REVEALS

Austin has mastered the art of interviews. Back when he was a newbie on YouTube, he got comfortable answering fans' questions. So, when he exploded on the music scene, he was already an old hand at the Q&A format. Austin loves a good up-close-and-personal question session, and here he goes from the silly to the serious. Does he explain the things you want to know?

On his most special possession . . . "I have this cross that I take with me everywhere I go. I sleep with it under my pillow. My grandma [gave it to me] when I was [little.]"

On being backstage with Taylor Swift during her Red Tour . . . "Taylor has this thing called Club Red—all the fans are there and we go around, take pictures, and just hang out. It's a really cool, chill vibe. I got a couple pictures with me, her, and Ed [Sheeran] in the photo booth, so it was really cool."

On his most-asked fan question on Twitter . . .

"Will you follow me?"

On his most embarrassing moment . . . "I was

learning how to water-ski and somehow my swim trunks, like, just came off. I don't know how it happened. They didn't rip. My skis were on, so I don't know how it even happened!"

On his favorite cover song . . . "I'd say 'Let Me

Love You' by Mario. It's one of my favorite songs of all time to cover."

Mario is one of Austin's all-time favorite singers and a major influence.

On his most romantic date . . .

"One time in my hometown, San Antonio in Texas, we have the Tower of the Americas. It's this giant tower, which is really skinny, and at the top it's got a restaurant that revolves. It was Christmastime and I took the girl up there for dinner, then I walked her around the whole downtown area. It was pretty cool."

San Antonio's Tower of the Americas is a favorite date-night spot for Austin.

On the time a crush broke his heart . . . "I said
something to a crush, but, well, it didn't go so well. We were friends—not best friends, but just, you know, friends. And I just told her, 'I like you as more than a friend.' My crush was like, 'You know, I like you, too, but I think we should just be friends.' I was heartbroken."

On how he chills after a performance . . . "To be
honest, I know this probably sounds corny or whatever because I'm a musician, but listening to music really helps me relax and calm down—listening to my favorite songs. Also laughing and hanging out with my friends."

On the most outrageous gift he has ever received from a fan . . . "There was this one time I said I needed a new chair because my chair was really squeaky and really annoying, and someone sent me an office chair. I thought it was from one of my managers. I was like, 'Thanks guys. I really appreciate it. It really means a lot.' And then they were like, 'What are you talking about? We didn't send you anything.' Then I found out it was from a fan. I was like, 'Wow, that was pretty nice.'"

Fandemonium for the Mahomies!

On the best part of being Austin Mahone . . .

"It's been amazing so far. Getting to travel and go to new countries and meeting people and making music and winning the VMA! Also going to perform for President Obama! . . . He was really cool! The whole family was really nice—I met his daughters and the dog [Bo]. . . . Very nice dog. He wasn't facing the camera, though. I got a picture and his butt was facing the camera!"

On the perks of turning 18 . . . "When I'm 18, I can

finally order that paid programming stuff on TV. Like it always says, 'Must be 18 or older to call,' so I'll be able to call! I can finally buy some blenders from the TV."

On the first time he heard himself on the radio . . . "I was in Chicago leaving a

radio show, and I got in the car . . . and I heard my voice. I was like, 'Hey, what's up, it's Austin Mahone. You're listening to B96.' And it was so weird. I didn't know what to do. It was strange."

On his life motto . . . "I have it on my

phone. It's my screen saver. 'Make the most of every opportunity because you only get one chance.' So, I want to take advantage of that."

AUSTIN'S MASHUP OF FUN!

BEHIND-THE-SCENES INFO

AUSTIN'S FOOD FAVES

RESTAURANT CHAIN
Olive Garden

TYPE OF FOOD
Italian—"Pizza is my favorite, but I like ziti. Lasagna's good, too. I like chicken Alfredo."

TEXAS RESTAURANT
Whataburger

BREAKFAST FOOD
Waffles

SANDWICH
Ham and cheese on Italian bread

SOUP
Chicken noodle

CONDIMENT
Ketchup

SODA
Dr Pepper

ICE CREAM FLAVOR
Chocolate and cookie dough

GUILTY DELIGHT
Chocolate peanut butter Pop-Tarts

AUSTIN'S CELEB ICONS

Taylor Swift:
"She always tells me to stay the kid I was when I was starting out on YouTube. She is so great. She's super talented and always puts on a good show. I learned a lot from her."

Drake:
"He's one of my biggest inspirations for music. He's an amazing artist. He speaks his mind and he keeps it real, so I'd like to do a collaboration with Drake."

Selena Gomez:
"She's real cool, she's real sweet, real nice. We're friends and she's always there for me, too."

Pitbull:
"He's wild, but actually really nice, really down to earth and very smart. He looks out for me."

Shoe Man
"The right sneaker makes me dance better. I can be on my toes better and spin on them."

FIRST ALBUM BOUGHT
Rascal Flatts

FIRST KISS
Underwater

FIRST GIRLFRIEND
Emily, when they were in kindergarten

FIRST PET
A sheltie named Angel

AUSTIN BEHIND THE WHEEL

When Austin turned 18, he was ready for every teen's rite of passage: getting his driver's license. It didn't go so well the first time—or the second time.

"It's pretty embarrassing. I went the first time, and I got in the car and I was singing. And the lady got mad at me. She said, 'Excuse me, can you stop singing?' So I said OK, and I started driving, and this is the part where I failed. There was a huge fire lane, and I'm pulling out, and I pulled straight through it and started driving—and she said, 'You failed.' . . . Now the second time, OK, I have a Range Rover. And I have the screen thing, so I'm backing up and I didn't know I was supposed to turn around, because my screen shows me where I'm backing up. So I'm not even looking behind me, and he failed me. The third time I passed!"

AUSTIN, THE HAT-SOME GUY

"I don't like the way my hair looks, so I wear a hat all the time," Austin explains. Check out some of his favorites . . .

WHAT DOES THE FUTURE HOLD FOR AUSTIN?

HARD WORK, MEGA GOALS, SUPER FANS WILL GET HIM THERE!

W ork until your idols become your rivals," is a saying Austin truly believes. Why? Well, according to a conversation Austin had with *J-14*, "when your idols become your rivals, you know you've worked hard and made it."

Austin understood the business side of the music industry. When record labels started to seek him out, Austin had talent, dedication, and a solid fan base.

Austin doesn't take it for granted. He appreciates every moment—from the hard work to the glamour of showbiz. "My life has changed in many ways," he told musichel.com. "I get to travel all over the world and I get to meet amazing people."

Austin is on a mission to grow as an artist. "You get only one chance, and you have to make the most of every opportunity," Austin told TeenVogue.com. "I want to look back and be like, 'Man, I killed that.'"

Now Austin is only thinking about a new album, a world tour, and a more impressive show. "We're working bigger venues, so there's more room to try new things," he told *USA Today*. But when musichel.com asked Austin about the future, he answered, "In 15 years, I see myself traveling across the world, putting out albums and still making music."

That's a prediction you can count on!

"I'LL NEVER GIVE UP ON MY DREAMS. NO MATTER WHAT!"

Resources

BOOKS

Mahone, Austin. *Just How It Happened: My Official Story.* New York: Little, Brown Books for Young Readers, 2014.

Schwartz, Heather E. *Austin Mahone: Vocals Going Viral.* Minneapolis: Lerner Publications, 2015.

Facts for Now

Visit this Scholastic Web site for more information on **Austin Mahone**
www.factsfornow.scholastic.com
Enter the keywords **Austin Mahone**

Glossary

covers *(KUHV-urz)* versions of songs made popular by other performers

EP *(EE PEE)* short for "extended play," an EP is shorter than a full album but longer than a single

gigs *(GIGZ)* live concerts

producers *(proh-DOOS-urz)* people who oversee the recording of a song or album

vlogs *(VLAHGZ)* video blogs

Index

Acknowledgments

Page 6: Growing up: *J-14* April 2014
Page 8: Presents: *J-14* April 2014; Mom's advice: JustJaredJr.com February 28, 2013; Drums: Scholastic STACKS July 13, 2012
Page 9: Confidence: *Twist* March 2013
Page 10: Friends: *PopStar* November 2012; YouTube King: Twist.com; First video: *Details* June/July 2013
Page 11: School hallways: *Details* June/July 2013
Page 12: Cheerleader request: *Twist* December 2012; Texas: *J-14* April 2014
Page 14: Twitter/Facebook: *Hollywood Reporter* June 6, 2013
Page 16: Skype: *Hollywood Reporter* June 6, 2013; Amazing fans: 4Music.com April 21, 2013
Page 19: Being genuine: *Hollywood Reporter* June 15, 2013

Page 20: Getting antsy: *Hollywood Reporter* June 15, 2013; Every song perfect: MTV News April 3, 2014
Page 21: Justin Bieber: *Details* June/July 2012
Page 23: Meeting Justin Bieber: Celebuzz.com June 26, 2012; Success: *Elvis Duran & The Morning Show* 2012
Page 25: Taylor Swift tour: *Elvis Duran & The Morning Show* 2012
Page 26: Performing in front of a crowd: JustJaredJr.com February 28, 2013; Artist To Watch: MTV News October 17, 2013
Page 27: Drake Tweet: Twitter/JustJaredJr.com August 26, 2013
Page 28: MTV Artist To Watch tour: MTV News October 17, 2013; Twitter/MTV News October 18, 2013

Page 29: Getting Better: *J-14* January 2014
Page 30: EMAs: TeenVogue.com November 2013
Page 31: Release of album: MTV News/Twitter April 4, 2014
Page 33: Special Possession: *Hollywood Life* June 2012; Red Tour: *J-14* August 2013
Page 34: Fan question: Scholastic STACKS June 2, 2012; Embarrassing moment: Scholastic STACKS June 2, 2012; Cover song: Bestfan.com December 5, 2012
Page 35: Romantic date: *Teen Now* October 2013; Crush: *Twist* January 2013; Chills: *Huffington Post* July 18, 2013
Page 36: Outrageous gift: *J-14* April 2013
Page 37: Being Austin Mahone: Buzzfeed.com 2014; Perks: Buzzfeed.com 2014;

On the radio: *Huffington Post* July 18, 2013; Motto: Miss O & Friends March 15, 2013
Page 39: Fave food/Italian: Scholastic STACKS July 13, 2012
Page 40: Taylor Swift: OMG.yahoo August 2, 2013; Drake: MTV News October 14, 2013; Selena Gomez: Femalefirst.co.uk March 22, 2014; Pitbull: *USA Today* May 29, 2014
Page 41: Shoe Man: *Bop* April 2014
Page 42: Behind the Wheel: Buzzfeed.com 2014
Page 43: Hat-Some guy: *Bop* 2013
Page 45: Idols/Rivals: *J-14* May/June 2014; Life change: musichel.com March 21, 2013; Never give up: *J-14* May/June 2014

About the Author

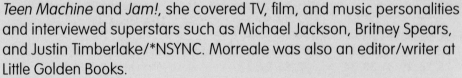

Marie Morreale is the author of many official and unofficial celebrity biographies. She attended New York University as an English/creative writing major and began her writing and editorial career in New York City. As the editor of teen/music magazines *Teen Machine* and *Jam!*, she covered TV, film, and music personalities and interviewed superstars such as Michael Jackson, Britney Spears, and Justin Timberlake/*NSYNC. Morreale was also an editor/writer at Little Golden Books.

Today, she is the executive editor, Media, of Scholastic Classroom Magazines writing about pop-culture, sports, news, and special events. Morreale lives in New York City and is entertained daily by her two Maine coon cats, Cher and Sullivan.